Danny –

...(the longer trip?)
is done, we'll
take our leave and
go.
♡Isabelle

Some day when

The Book of
Sea Shanties

The Book of Sea Shanties

Wellerman *and* Other Songs
from the Seven Seas

Nathan Evans

WELBECK

Published by Welbeck
An imprint of Welbeck Non-Fiction Limited,
part of Welbeck Publishing Group.
20 Mortimer Street,
London W1T 3JW

First published by Welbeck in 2021

Copyright © Nathan Evans, 2021

Nathan Evans has asserted his right under the
Copyright, Designs and Patents Act, 1988, to be identified
as Author of this work.

All rights reserved. No part of this publication may be reproduced,
stored in a retrieval system, or transmitted in any form or by any
means, electronically, mechanical, photocopying, recording or
otherwise, without the prior permission of the copyright owners
and the publishers.

A CIP catalogue record for this book is available
from the British Library

ISBN Hardback – 9781787399587

Typeset by Roger Walker

Printed in Great Britain by CPI Books, Croydon, CR0 4YY

10 9 8 7 6 5 4 3 2 1

The Forest Stewardship Council® is an international nongovernmental
organization that promotes environmentally appropriate, socially
beneficial, and economically viable management of the world's forests.
To learn more, visit www.fsc.org

www.welbeckpublishing.com

'What makes a shantyman sing?' words by Ben Morgan

Lyrics to 'Ring Ding (A Scotsman's Story)' and 'Told You So'
reproduced with kind permission from Warner Chappell Music.

The following shanties reflect the time they were written in
and may include language no longer in use today.

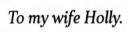

To my wife Holly.

CONTENTS

What makes a shantyman sing?

Wind, driving rain, bitter cold. A lone call goes up, shimmering on the spray of waves. Seconds later, the voice of a ship-full of sea-farers answers. In deep, thrumming rhythms, the shanty begins.

Rhythm is the heart of the sea. Waves pulse on the hull like heartbeats, wind sings through the ropes and pulleys, lone seabirds tear the air with their cries, and as the weary sailors haul, heave, hoist or run the capstan, these beats run through them into song. Shanties, as spontaneous as a sudden gust in the sails, as old as the ships and seas that engendered them, marry improvisation with tradition, call with response, lament with celebration. With one eye over the shoulder to the shore, the lands, the lovers they've left behind and the other toward the ever-receding horizon, these tales carry the sailors on, carving a path through barren, turbulent oceans, dreaming of return.

ACKNOWLEDGEMENTS

There are so many people I would like to thank for making this journey possible. It's been an incredible ride and I'm so grateful to everyone who's helped me get here.

To my amazing family: thank you for all your love and support. I could never have done this without you.

My phenomenal team have helped me every step of the way; in particular my thanks go to Dakota Hoven from Chosen Music and my agent Professor Jonathan Shalit OBE from InterTalent Group. Thank you for making this book possible.

I would like to thank the team at Welbeck Publishing. My thanks go to Ajda Vucicevic, Millie Acers, Rachel Burgess, Clare Hennessy, Lyndsey Mayhew, Annabel Robinson, as well as Nico Poilblanc and the entire sales team. A special thank you to Shone Abhyankar from ED Public Relations.

This book would not be possible or look as good as it does without the fantastic and the very talented Alexandra Allden and Sally Taylor. I am particularly indebted to Roger

Walker for working his magic to make this book into what you're holding today. Thank you again.

Finally, a big thank you to George Robarts for working with me on this book and helping me put it together. It's been such a pleasure to do so.

I hope you enjoy reading this book as much as I've enjoyed writing it. Love, Nathan x.

INTRODUCTION

It was a Friday morning in early January, and the bitter cold was doing its best to crush my spirits as I left my parents' house and headed for the central post office. Scotland had just gone into another lockdown, and the snow-covered streets felt a little emptier than usual on my way in to work. Postmen like me were still out and about every morning, but most people were confined to their homes and nothing seemed certain any more.

And on this particular Friday morning, life felt stranger than ever. There was something about today that was noticeably different. The few faces I passed on the street held my eye for just a second longer than usual. A couple on the other side of the street turned to look as I went by with my postbag. And I couldn't help noticing some excited whispers from strangers as I passed.

"Is that–?"

"Yes! I think it is!"

I tried to concentrate on my work, without letting myself get too distracted. But I couldn't help thinking, *This is it. This has to be it.* There was something in the air. And I had to seize it while it lasted.

I thought back to the previous day. My phone had been pinging all through my shift, with excited messages from friends and family. They'd seen the video I'd posted to TikTok of me singing a centuries-old, little-known whaling song from New Zealand – and they had watched with astonishment as it spread like wildfire across the internet. Suddenly, almost overnight, I'd become some sort of viral star. And later that day, just when I thought it couldn't get any crazier, my phone had rung again.

"Hello?"

"Hello, is that Nathan Evans?"

"Yeah, that's right. Who's this?"

"Hello, Mr Evans, I'm calling from Polydor Records."

My head span. "Poly–? Polydor Records? Ok. Right. Polydor? As in... *Polydor*?"

"That's us! We've been loving your videos, Nathan, and we've got a proposal that I'd like to discuss with you if you've got a minute..."

That call had been the most surreal experience of my life. Here I was, going about my rounds just as I had done each day for what seemed like an eternity. On the surface, everything looked the same as ever. And yet nothing was the same. I was pushing letters through doors in my red jacket like any other Friday, but suddenly I had an offer of a recording contract on the table from an iconic record label.

As I turned a corner, lost in my own thoughts, I nearly bumped into two kids and their dad, who was taking them out to play in the snow. They gasped excitedly and their eyes widened.

"Are you the man that sings the sea shanties?"

"Are you the Wellerman man?"

I grinned. "Yeah, that's me, I'm Nathan. Nice to meet you. How are you doing?"

"Can we have a photo?" they asked delightedly.

I didn't know where to look. Since when did people stop me in the street for photo ops? I nodded shyly and stood with them as their dad took our picture. We chatted briefly, and I went on my way, heading for the next door along.

It was then that it hit me. This was a golden opportunity that I just had to take. I had no choice – this had to be my last day as a postman. I went to see my boss, and told him everything that had been going on behind the scenes. My life had changed drastically in so little time. He agreed it was time for me to spread my wings and go for it.

The following weeks were a haze. I could hardly believe any of it was real. I signed my deal with Polydor, I was invited to perform the One Show, and I even appeared on Good Morning America.

But most incredibly of all, a few weeks later in March 2021, my sea shanty cover "Wellerman" hit the top of the UK charts.

How on earth had I got here? It was all thanks to a song that barely anyone had heard of until a few weeks before. A song first sung over 150 years ago on the other side of the globe.

Sea shanties are a tradition that had pretty much disappeared from the modern world. They no longer seemed to serve any purpose beyond their historical interest. But suddenly, in 2021, this niche genre had captured the imagination of millions of people. What was it about the sea shanty that hit the mark?

The first part of the answer seems obvious: they're just so much fun. Fun to sing, fun to listen to, and fun to join in with. When I made that appearance on the One Show, Alex Jones said that shanties "remind everyone of being in a pub". We were going through the worst of the pandemic so far, and these songs, with their simple, catchy tunes and thumping rhythms, were providing just the kind of morale boost and sense of community that we all needed. It had been a brutal winter – people were lonely and separated from their loved ones – and all anyone wanted was to get together, sing some songs and have a good time. We were all stuck at home, but the shanty was the perfect feel-good music for people to join in with remotely, duetting with each other on online platforms all over the world.

But here's the strange thing: sea shanties were never meant to be sung for fun. For thousands of years, shanties were working songs, whose main purpose was to help a ship's crew carry out heavy-duty manual labour more efficiently. Seamen on merchant ships would sing shanties when hauling ropes to raise the sails, or pushing bars round an enormous winch to raise the anchor. The crew all had to push or pull at the same time to make their task easier – and singing a shanty chorus was an ideal way to co-ordinate their efforts. The whole crew would push or pull on a strong beat in the music, and the physical exertion of singing would support the physical effort of their work.

Shanties accompanied hours of tedious manual labour, and they were so vital to a crew's work that often there was a crew member specially appointed to lead the singing. The shantyman would start the song with a solo verse, and the crew would respond with the chorus as they heaved (pushed) or hauled (pulled). Then the shantyman would sing another verse, and the crew would repeat the chorus as they strained once more.

So, next time you get one of those catchy choruses in your head, take a moment to imagine how it must have felt to be singing it on deck, out on the stormy seas, with hours of toil and sweat ahead.

That said, shanties were important aboard ship for other reasons too. Crews could be out at sea for months at a time, often with poor food supplies, bad pay, and rough weather conditions to contend with. So they needed some way of keeping their spirits up on a day-to-day basis. Sea shanties not only made sailors' work physically easier, but they were also a way for the crew to pull together as a unit, transforming gruelling labour into something more. They built team spirit and added a degree of amusement to hours of mundane work.

Shanties were sung differently on every ship, and the shantyman often invented new verses on the spot to tailor a song to the crew and their specific situation. Perhaps he would complain about their low wages, or the terrible food the sailors had to endure (it was a diet high in biscuits, because they never went off) – or he would poke fun at some mistake a shipmate had made the previous day. This increased the sense of camaraderie on board, giving the crew a way to let off steam about their working conditions. They would always respond with the same chorus line, so as not to interrupt the task at hand, but the shantyman would carry on making up fresh verses to keep them entertained.

The song continued until the job was done, meaning that sea shanties could be as long or short as they needed to be. Shanties typically have lots and lots of different verses to choose from, with endless scope for variation and improvisation – so it's only possible to provide a small selection of my favourites in this book. (Most of the examples here were sung around two hundred years ago, before the age of automation and mechanisation, when shanty singing was still a way of life out on the high seas.)

So, unusually for today's listeners, there is no single definitive version of any sea shanty. Words were improvised depending on the situation, and the rhythms and speeds of the songs varied depending on the type of work being done. One shanty was never sung the same way twice – so the shanties in this book are all songs that you can truly make your own. There's no single "original" version of a sea shanty.

At a personal level, it's still amazing to me how far *Wellerman's* success has reached beyond the UK. Shanties have never been a mainstream genre – even back in their heyday, they were only ever heard at sea – and even for English-speakers, their language is often hard to understand. Until December 2020, most of us didn't even know that "Wellerman" was a word!

But perhaps the unfamiliar language of shanties is part of what's made them internationally popular. The sea shanty ultimately had its origins in slave songs, and as history progressed, different shanties drew on a mix of cultures, traditions, places, stories and languages. After all, ships stopped off in countries all over the world, and one sailor could absorb stories and vocabulary from across the globe over the course of a lifetime. Crews were often made up of sailors from different countries, who spoke different languages – so the nautical language that you hear in the shanties was essentially born out of their mish-mash of international experiences. But there was one common language that all sailors shared: the language of music and song. And that's a language we all still share today.

What drew me to sea shanties as a genre was the pure spontaneity of the music – the stripped-back acoustic rawness of voices singing together unaccompanied. I also love the spirit of optimism that they foster. And that spirit is surely what turned the shanty into a lockdown sensation. Sea shanties used to provide a sense of community and entertainment in mundane situations out at sea – and this year, they rediscovered that purpose. The sense of togetherness they create is something truly valuable, and I hope that the shanty will stay with us beyond the pandemic. In less troubled times, they will keep reminding us how lucky we are to be all together again.

THE SHANTIES

Note: Shanty lyrics printed in *italics* were sung in unison by the ship's crew. Straight text indicates lines sung by a soloist (the shantyman), who led the song. The most common shanty structure contains alternating verses and choruses: the shantyman sang verses alone, while the choruses took a call-and-response form between the shantyman and crew.

THE SHANTIES

ROLL THE OLD CHARIOT ALONG

Oh, a drop of Nelson's blood wouldn't do us
any harm
*Oh, a drop of Nelson's blood wouldn't do us any
harm*
Oh, a drop of Nelson's blood wouldn't do us
any harm
And we'll all hang on behind

Chorus:
So we'll roll the old chariot along
So we'll roll the old chariot along
So we'll roll the old chariot along
And we'll all hang on behind!

Oh, a plate of Irish stew wouldn't do us any
harm
Oh, a plate of Irish stew wouldn't do us any harm
Oh, a plate of Irish stew wouldn't do us any
harm
And we'll all hang on behind

Chorus

Oh, a nice fat cook wouldn't do us any harm
Oh, a nice fat cook wouldn't do us any harm
Oh, a nice fat cook wouldn't do us any harm
And we'll all hang on behind

Chorus

Oh, a roll in the clover wouldn't do us any
   harm
Oh, a roll in the clover wouldn't do us any harm
Oh, a roll in the clover wouldn't do us any
   harm
And we'll all hang on behind

Chorus

Oh, a long spell in the gaol wouldn't do us any
   harm
*Oh, a long spell in the gaol clover wouldn't do us any
   harm*
Oh, a long spell in the gaol wouldn't do us any
   harm
And we'll all hang on behind

Chorus

Oh, we'd be alright if we make it 'round the
    horn
Oh, we'd be alright if we make it 'round the horn
Oh, we'd be alright if we make it 'round the
    horn
And we'll all hang on behind

Chorus

Oh, we'd be alright if the wind was in our
    sails
Oh, we'd be alright if the wind was in our sails
Oh, we'd be alright if the wind was in our
    sails
And we'll all hang on behind

Chorus

Well, a night on the town wouldn't do us any
    harm
Well, a night on the town wouldn't do us any harm
Well, a night on the town wouldn't do us any
    harm
And we'll all hang on behind

Chorus

If the devil's in the way, we'll roll right over him
If the devil's in the way, we'll roll right over him
If the devil's in the way, we'll roll right over him
And we'll all hang on behind

Chorus

Oh, we'll be all right when the skipper's in his
     grave
Oh, we'll be all right when the skipper's in his grave
Oh, we'll be all right when the skipper's in his
     grave
And we'll all hang on behind

Chorus

This is a great song and a real morale-booster. The chorus is simple, uplifting and gets everyone singing along in an instant.

The beat moves at a spirited walking pace, making it the perfect accompaniment to tasks on ship that required steady physical effort. *Roll the Old Chariot* is a "capstan" shanty, meaning that it was sung while pushing heavy bars around the capstan, the central revolving drum that drew up the anchor.

There's plenty of irony in the lyrics, which complain about the sailors' life of labour and isolation with a wry smile. "Nelson's blood" is sailor slang for rum – because when Nelson died, he was supposedly transported back to Britain in a rum barrel to preserve his body.

Sailors would have longed for nothing more than a drink, a night in a comfy bed (preferably with company), a spell of better weather, or a more forgiving captain. There's a strong spirit of rowdiness and rebellion here against the monotony of life at sea, but the boisterous chorus gave sailors an opportunity to vent all their frustrations in rousing song.

There's so much life in this shanty, and it's one of my favourites to sing. There's a brilliant cover on YouTube by David Coffin, who performs it in the street in the middle of a crowd of people. They soon join in – that's just the effect it has. The tune never gets old, and everyone can belt it out together.

It was a perfect lockdown shanty for the same reasons that sailors sang it back in the day. We all needed to let off steam now and then while stuck at home – and we were all looking forward to getting the wind back in our sails!

SHENANDOAH

Oh Shenandoah, I long to see you
Away, you rolling river
Oh Shenandoah, I long to see you
Way, we're bound away across the wide Missouri

Oh Shenandoah, I love your daughter
Away, you rolling river
For her I'd cross your roaming waters
Way, we're bound away across the wide Missouri

'Tis seven years since last I've seen you
Away, you rolling river
'Tis seven years since last I've seen you
Way, we're bound away across the wide Missouri

Oh Shenandoah, I long to hear you
Away, you rolling river
Oh Shenandoah, I long to hear you
Way, we're bound away across the wide Missouri

Oh Shenandoah, I long to hear you
Away, you rolling river
Oh Shenandoah, just to be near you
Way, we're bound away across the wide Missouri

One of the best-loved shanties out there – it's an American classic that's been performed and recorded by an endless list of stars. It paints a beautiful nostalgic picture of the Missouri river, where its story is set.

"Shenandoah" is a real historical person: John Skenandoa, who was an Oneida (Native American) chief. He was a significant figure in the Seven Years' War and the American War of Independence, and commanded respect from all sides. He lived past the

ripe old age of 100, dying in 1816. The Shenandoah river, valley and mountain are named after him – as are several towns, counties, and neighbourhoods across the US.

The original song's lyrics are about a settler who falls in love with Shenandoah's daughter and wants to marry her. A verse from an early rendition of the song goes like this: "The white man loved the Indian maiden, Away you rolling river..." The Missouri was a favoured route for beaver fur traders who plied the river by canoe, and the "white man" in the song was probably one of these traders.

Shenandoah was first sung along the waters of the Missouri, but was later adopted by sailors on cargo and passenger boats on the Mississippi river. From there, it spread out into the oceans, adapted into a capstan shanty that sailors sang while heaving in the anchor.

With its haunting, rolling melody, *Shenandoah* has survived well beyond the end of the shanty era, and has taken on a life all of its own. It's hard to believe that such a relaxing tune was once used to accompany hard labour, but I suppose its enduring popularity as a beautiful ballad is just one of many weird and wonderful curiosities of the shanty tradition.

LOWLANDS AWAY

I dreamed a dream the other night
Lowlands, lowlands away, my John
I dreamed a dream the other night
Lowlands, lowlands away

I dreamed I saw my own true love
Lowlands, lowlands away, my John
I dreamed I saw my own true love
Lowlands, lowlands away

He was green and wet with weeds so cold
Lowlands, lowlands away, my John
He was green and wet with weeds so cold
Lowlands, lowlands away

All dank his hair, all dim his eye
Lowlands, lowlands away, my John
I knew that he had said goodbye
Lowlands, lowlands away

"I'm drowned in the Lowland Sea," he said
Lowlands, lowlands away, my John
"Oh, you and I will ne'er be wed"
Lowlands, lowlands away

I'll cut away my bonny hair
Lowlands, lowlands away, my John
For no other man shall think me fair
Lowlands, lowlands away

For my love lies drowned in the windy lowlands
Lowlands, lowlands away, my John
For my love lies drowned in the windy lowlands
Lowlands, lowlands away

The unusual nature of this shanty comes from the fact that it pictures the sailor's life from the perspective not of the sailor himself, but of a loved one who he's left behind. It's beautifully melancholic – the tune is slow and reflective, and the words are devastating – making it one of the most moving shanties out there.

Lowlands Away brings home the very real fears that a sailor's family had to face every time he went to sea. Each voyage brought grave danger. The awful prospect of a sailor being swept away in a storm really was too close for comfort.

The lyrics recount a woman's vision of her husband or boyfriend in a dream. She calls him "my John" – slang for a common sailor on a merchant ship. His ship has been away in the lowlands, and he now appears before her, covered in weeds, to give her the terrible news that he has drowned. It is uncertain which "lowlands" he has died in, but the Caribbean,

Scotland and the Netherlands are just a few possibilities here.

Lowlands Away is sung in fairly free time, without the thumping beat you might usually expect from a shanty. The melody gently rises and falls through each phrase, lending the song its sorrowful, heart-rending quality. There's a beautiful rendition of this shanty sung by a group called The Corries – look it up, you won't regret it.

A LONG TIME AGO

A long, long time, and a long time ago
To me way, hay, oh-hi-oh!
A long, long time, and a long time ago
A long time ago!

A smart Yankee packet lay out in the bay
To me way, hay, oh-hi-oh!
Awaiting for a fair wind to get under way
A long time ago!

With all her poor sailors sick and all sad
To me way, hay, oh-hi-oh!
For they'd drunk all their whiskey, no more
could be had
A long time ago!

She was waiting for a fair wind to get under way
To me way, hay, oh-hi-oh!
If she hasn't had a fair wind she's lying there still
A long time ago!

A dollar a day is a stevedore's pay
To me way, hay, oh-hi-oh!
Dollar a day, I heard them say
A long time ago!

I bought in Hong Kong a pretty silk dress
To me way, hay, oh-hi-oh!
I'm taking it home to my sweetheart Bess
A long time ago!

My Bess is fair and sweet to view
To me way, hay, oh-hi-oh!
Her hair is brown and her eyes are blue
A long time ago!

I thought I heard our second mate say
To me way, hay, oh-hi-oh!
One more pull, and then belay
A long time ago!

In the days before mechanisation, ships couldn't just set sail whenever the captain felt like it – they had to wait for fair weather. Without today's enormous engines and automatic machinery, sea travel was a very different prospect.

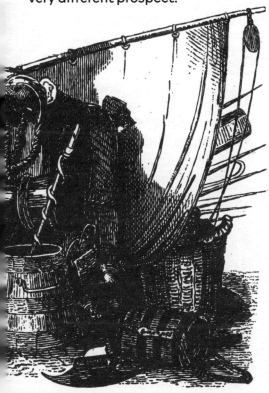

This shanty tells us what it was like for sailors to be kept waiting around, using up their precious supplies, as weeks of bad weather prevented their ship from leaving port. It sounds pretty monotonous and demoralising to me. But this shanty, with its simple, rocking melody and swung chorus, transforms the experience into something worth remembering.

A Long Time Ago is what's known as a "halyard" shanty or a "long-drag" shanty. This means it was sung to accompany tasks that required pulling, rather than pushing. Setting the sails, for example, required hauling away at ropes for an extended period of time. Halyard shanties typically emphasised two syllables in the chorus line – A *long* time a-*go* – as the crew pulled on the ropes twice in quick succession, with all their might.

Hauling tasks like setting the sails could take an age, so there are many, many verses and versions of this shanty out there. The final verse printed here is a final encouragement from the shantyman for one last big pull before the crew "belays" (fixes the sail in place) and sets off again.

DRUNKEN SAILOR

What shall we do with the drunken sailor?
What shall we do with the drunken sailor?
What shall we do with the drunken sailor?
Early in the morning

Chorus:
Way hey and up she rises
Way hey and up she rises
Way hey and up she rises
Early in the morning

Shave his belly with a rusty razor
Shave his belly with a rusty razor
Shave his belly with a rusty razor
Early in the morning

Chorus

Put him in a longboat till he's sober
Put him in a longboat till he's sober
Put him in a longboat till he's sober
Early in the morning

Chorus

Put him in the bilge and make him drink it
Put him in the bilge and make him drink it
Put him in the bilge and make him drink it
Early in the morning

Chorus

Put him in the scuppers with a hose-pipe
   on him
Put him in the scuppers with a hose-pipe on him
Put him in the scuppers with a hose-pipe
   on him
Early in the morning

Chorus

Take 'im and shake 'im and try an' wake 'im
Take 'im and shake 'im and try an' wake 'im
Take 'im and shake 'im and try an' wake 'im
Early in the morning

Chorus

32

One of the best-loved shanties out there – this is one I've known for years.

Discipline was tight in the nineteenth century, and turning up for work drunk was as frowned upon then as it is now. But there wasn't much point in sacking a disorderly crew member when you were out at sea with nowhere else for him to go. So this jaunty-sounding shanty suggests a number of grisly punishments that could be inflicted on him aboard ship instead.

If being shaved with a rusty razor doesn't sound unpleasant enough, the idea of drinking bilge water is enough to turn your stomach. The "bilge" of a ship is the bottom part of its inner hull, where water (rainwater, sea spray and leakages) would collect and stagnate. Mixed up with the dirt and grime from the ship's hull, the water would turn foul and sludgy. After whatever the drunken sailor's been drinking, a cup of bilgewater would certainly be a nasty shock to the system.

Another suggested punishment is to lie the drunken sailor down in the "scuppers" –openings at the side of

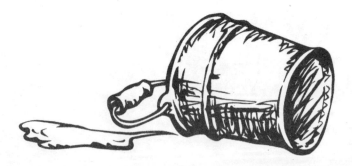

the ship that allowed any water that collected on deck to drain away into the sea. The hosepipe to spray him down with was used to pump water out of the bilges – another nasty outcome for anyone who stepped out of line!

Sung in a minor key to a pulsing beat and spiky semiquaver rhythms, I think there's an element of morbid glee involved in singing about all these nasty punishments. It's a shanty I love to sing, and it's definitely one to get the crowd going. The pace of the song never lets up, and people always know it and can join in.

JOHNNY'S GONE TO HILO

My Johnny's gone, what shall I do?
My Johnny's gone to Hilo
And if he says so I'll go too
My Johnny's gone to Hilo

Hilo, a-Hilo
My Johnny's gone to Hilo
My Johnny's gone and I'll go too
My Johnny's gone to Hilo

My Johnny's sailed away to sea
My Johnny's gone to Hilo
A mermaid's lover he'll surely be
My Johnny's gone to Hilo

My Johnny's sailed from off of these shores
My Johnny's gone to Hilo
I'll never see my Johnny no more
My Johnny's gone to Hilo

Like *Lowlands Away*, *Johnny's Gone to Hilo* is a shanty about the loved ones who sailors left behind when they went to sea. It gives voice to the fear that a sailor's wife or girlfriend would have felt – the fear that he might never return.

The descending melody in the verses perfectly conveys the desolation and loneliness of those left behind. In the chorus, "My Johnny's *gone*..." is sung over a rising major sixth, a particularly expressive musical interval that sounds just like a sigh.

This shanty was first sung in the Americas: "Hilo" is an Anglicisation of the port of Ilo, on the west coast of Peru. It is thought to be of African-American origin, and appeared in a variety of versions (Johnny is sometimes referred to as Tommy instead).

The idea that Johnny might become a "mermaid's lover" partly expresses the concern that a sailor might meet another lover in faraway lands and choose not to return. But becoming a "mermaid's lover" at the bottom of the ocean is also a heart-breaking allusion to the possibility of a sailor drowning at sea – one of the most beautiful and gut-wrenching images in any shanty.

ROLL, BULLIES, ROLL

From Liverpool to 'Frisco a-roving I went
For to stay in that country was my good intent
But drinking strong whiskey like other damn
   fools
Oh, I was very soon shanghaied to Liverpool

Chorus:
Singing roll, roll, roll bullies, roll!
Them Liverpool Judies have got us in tow

I shipped in near Lasker lying out in the bay
We were waiting for a fair wind to get under
   way
The sailors on board they were all sick and sore
They'd drunk all their whiskey and couldn't get
   no more

Chorus

One night off Cape Horn I will never forget
And it's oh but a sigh when I think of it yet
We were going bows under with her sailors
   all wet
She was running twelve knots with her main
   skysail set

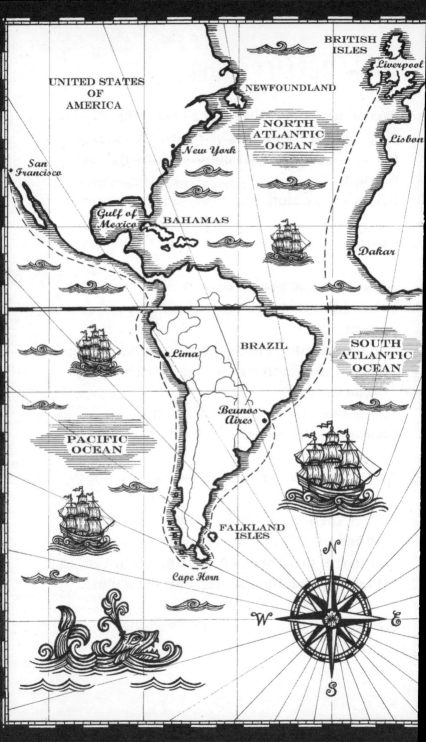

Well along comes the mate in his jacket o' blue
He's looking for work for them outlaws to do
Oh, it's "Up tops and higher!" he loudly does
    roar
And it's "Lay aloft Paddy, ye son of a-whore!"

Chorus

And now we are sailing down onto the line
When I think of it now, oh we've had a hard
    time
The sailors box-hauling them yards all around
To catch that flash clipper the Thatcher
    MacGowan

Chorus

And now we've arrived in the Bramleymoor
    dock
And all them flash Judies on the pierhead do
    flock
Our barrel's run dry and my six quid advance
I think it's high time for to get up and dance

Chorus

Here's a health to our captain wherever he
    may be
He's a devil on land and a bucko at sea
But as for the first mate, that lousy old brute
We hope when he dies straight to hell he'll
    skyhoot

Chorus

This shanty is a cautionary tale about drinking too much. Sung in three time, it has the feel of a drinking song, with a carefree, swinging rhythm that sounds like a sailor stumbling around town.

As the story goes, a sailor arrives in San Francisco ("Frisco") after the long journey from Liverpool. He decides to stay in the city and start a new life there. But during a night out on the booze, he wakes up to find he's been "Shanghaied" – dragged aboard another ship while he was too drunk to know anything about it. This practice of forced conscription was eventually outlawed, but it was widespread in the nineteenth century in parts of the US.

As in any good shanty, the chorus puts a positive spin on this rather depressing turn of events. "Them Liverpool Judies have got us in tow" is another way of saying "We can't stay away from the Liverpool women". ("Judy" is archaic Scouse slang for a young woman, and "flash Judies" means the sailors' girlfriends, who they hope will be waiting for them when the ship arrives back in Liverpool.)

This shanty was sung on cargo ships crossing the Atlantic on trade routes between Liverpool and the US, with destinations including San Francisco and New York. Crews starting out from Liverpool would often include many Irish sailors, and it's thought that this shanty has Irish roots (the name "Paddy" is a clue in verse 4).

The song also reveals the extraordinary length of some of the sea voyages that sailors endured. The only way of getting from San Francisco back to Liverpool in those days was by sailing all the way down the west coast of North and South America, rounding Cape Horn at the southern tip of Chile (verse 3), before heading out into the Atlantic to cross the equator for a second time in a single voyage ("the line" in verse 5 means the equator).

Imagine doing that journey one way, and then finding you're being forced to do all it all again in reverse – just because you had one too many whiskeys and blacked out for a while.

HEAVE AWAY

Come get your duds in order 'cause we're
bound to cross the water
Heave away, me Johnnies, heave away
Come get your duds in order 'cause we're
bound to leave tomorrow
*Heave away, me Johnny boys, we're all
bound away*

Sometimes we're bound for
Liverpool, sometimes we're
bound for Spain
*Heave away, me Johnnies, heave
away*
But now we're bound for old
St John's where all the girls
are dancing
*Heave away, me Johnny boys,
we're all bound away*

There's some that's bound for New York town
    and some that's bound for France
Heave away, me Johnnies, heave away
But now we're bound for London town to
    teach the girls to dance
Heave away, me Johnny boys, we're all bound away

I wrote me love a letter, I was on the Jenny Lind
Heave away, me Johnnies, heave away
I wrote me love a letter, and I signed it with a ring
Heave away, me Johnny boys, we're all bound away

The day was fine when we set sail, the wind was
    blowing free
Heave away, me Johnnies, heave away
But soon afresh it blew a gale and we were far at
    sea
Heave away, me Johnny boys, we're all bound away

He shook her in the morning, oh the bosun was
    a-bawling
Heave away, me Johnnies, heave away
He shook her till the evening and the mast it was
    a-heaving
Heave away, me Johnny boys, we're all bound away

So it's farewell Nancy darlin', 'cause it's now I'm
    gonna leave you
Heave away, me Johnnies, heave away
You promised that you'd marry me, but how
    you did deceive me
Heave away, me Johnny boys, we're all bound away

This is a song I was lucky enough to duet on TikTok back in February 2021 with the one and only Alan Doyle, the inspirational Canadian folk singer. It is what's known as a windlass shanty. The windlass was another device used to raise the anchor, slightly different from the capstan (see *Roll the Old Chariot Along*). To operate the windlass, sailors pumped a hand-brake up and down in a see-saw like motion.

This pumping motion was steadier work than heaving bars around the capstan. Whereas capstan shanties typically emphasised one or two words in the chorus to coincide with shunting the bars forward, operating the windlass required less brute force and more sustained effort. You can hear this reflected in the song: *Heave Away* has a free-flowing melody, without such heavy emphasis on particular words making it well suited to the continuous physical movement of pumping the windlass. Its dotted rhythms give the shanty a real forward motion to it – a sense of excitement at what's to come.

The shanty itself tells the story of sailors packing their bags (their "duds") and setting out for far-flung lands, be it Spain, New York, or St John's on the eastern tip of Canada. Rhythmically, it's sprightly and upbeat, and there's a real sense of excitement at all the exotic destinations a sailor could be bound for on any given trip. But this song also shows us the sacrifices any sailor would be making as he went aboard – many girlfriends left behind, and there was no guarantee that the relationship would survive such a long separation.

SPANISH LADIES

Farewell and adieu unto you Spanish ladies
Farewell and adieu to you ladies of Spain
For we've received orders to sail for old
    England
But we hope very soon we shall see you again

Chorus:
We'll rant and we'll roar like true British sailors
We'll rant and we'll roar across the salt seas
Until we strike soundings in the Channel of Old
    England
From Ushant to Scilly is thirty-five leagues

We hove our ship to with the wind at sou'west,
    boys
We hove our ship to, our soundings to see
So we rounded and sounded; got forty-five
    fathoms
We squared our main yard and up channel
    steered we

Chorus

Now the first land we made it is called the
Deadman
Next Ram Head off Plymouth, off Portland the
Wight
We sailed by Beachy, by Fairlee and Dungeness
Till we came abreast of the South Foreland
Light

Chorus

Then the signal was made for the grand fleet to
  anchor
All in the Downs that night for to lie
Then it's stand by your stoppers, see clear your
  shank-painters
Haul all your clew garnets, let tacks and sheets
  fly

Chorus

Now let every man toss off a full bumper
And let every man drink off a full glass
And we'll drink and be merry and drown
  melancholy
Singing, here's a good health to each true-
  hearted lass

Chorus

This rousing tune started life as a British naval song. In the Royal Navy, very few songs were permitted, but this (along with *Drunken Sailor*) was one that made the cut. It was originally sung before the sea shanty tradition had taken hold – sea shanties were first sung not on navy ships, but on commercial ships carrying cargo and passengers across the seas. But once these commercial ships came along, their sailors soon adopted *Spanish Ladies* as a capstan shanty.

The bullish chorus is full of chest-beating and military aggression. "Ranting and roaring" might not seem like "true British" characteristics to us, but you can imagine this song getting a bunch of war-ready seaman pumped up and ready for action?!

Why are they singing goodbye to Spanish ladies? Well, between 1793 and 1796, Spain was fighting a war against Napoleon. Britain and France weren't exactly on the best of terms, so the Royal Navy sent supplies to Spain by ship. When the British crews arrived in Spain, many of them inevitably fell for Spanish women – and at the end of the war, they weren't able to take them home (because no Royal Navy captain was ever going to allow them on board).

The shanty itself tells the story of how the crew finds their way back from Spain. After travelling up the west coast of France, they aim to pass between the island of Ushant off the north-west tip of France and the Scilly Isles off the Cornish coast. But they get lost and have to work out where they are.

To establish their location, they "hove to" (stop the ship) and test their "soundings" (the depth of the water). They find that the sea is 45 fathoms deep – which tells them it's time to turn eastwards into the English Channel. The rest of the song checks off the landmarks up the south coast of Britain as they make their way home, docking in the light of the South Foreland Lighthouse, a historic landmark that towers over the white cliffs of Dover.

The crew may have left their Spanish sweethearts behind, but once they arrive back on land, they find plenty of time to celebrate their homecoming and drown their sorrows.

RUNNING DOWN TO CUBA

Running down to Cuba with a load of sugar
Weigh, me boys, to Cuba!
Make her run you lime juice squeezes
Running down to Cuba

O, I got a sister, she's nine feet tall
Weigh, me boys, to Cuba!
Sleeps in the kitchen with her feet in the hall
Running down to Cuba

The captain he will trim the sails
Weigh, me boys, to Cuba!
Winging the water over the rails
Running down to Cuba

Give me a gal can dance Fandango
Weigh, me boys, to Cuba!
Round as a melon and sweet as a mango
Running down to Cuba

Load this sugar and homeward go
Weigh, me boys, to Cuba!
Mister mate, he told me so
Running down to Cuba

This is a peculiar shanty: it wasn't used for work. Even stranger is the fact that it was very rarely sung to completion on ship.

Running Down to Cuba is essentially a protest shanty. Sailors sang it to show discontent and disobedience towards their superiors – they would suddenly launch into song, while stamping on deck in time to the words. It was an openly rebellious gesture to sing this shanty, so it was only rarely heard on board. And when it was, the officers would bark at the sailors to stop it immediately, or else there'd be trouble.

The tune is short, sharp and simple, with the chorus lines sung on an ascending arpeggio followed by a descending scale. It has the feel of a football or rugby chant – the chorus lines aren't far away from *Swing Low, Sweet Chariot*.

There's little rhyme or reason to the lyrics. Cuba was one of the largest sugar producers in the Caribbean, so it doesn't make much sense for a ship to be taking a load of sugar there. You might also be wondering what "lime juice squeezes" means in the third line. This is a reference to British sailors, who were known colloquially as "limeys" – because the Royal Navy gave their sailors citrus juice to prevent scurvy (a disease that was common at sea, resulting from vitamin C deficiency).

This is a fierce and fantastic shanty. When they were feeling really hard done by, sailors would sing as many of these verses as they could before the song was inevitably nipped in the bud.

SOUTH AUSTRALIA

In South Australia I was born
Heave away, haul away!
In South Australia, round Cape Horn
Bound for South Australia

Chorus:
Haul away you rolling kings
Heave away, haul away!
Haul away, you'll hear me sing
We're bound for South Australia

Now as I went out one morning fair
Heave away, haul away!
'Twas there I met Miss Nancy Blair
Bound for South Australia

Chorus

I shook her up, I shook her down
Heave away, haul away!
I shook her up and down the town
Bound for South Australia

Chorus

There ain't but one thing grieves my mind
Heave away, haul away!
It's to leave Miss Nancy Blair behind
Bound for South Australia

Chorus

And as we wallop around Cape Horn
Heave away, haul away!
You wish to God you'd never been born!
Bound for South Australia

Chorus

Imagine travelling to the opposite side of the world at a time when it could take up to 100 days to get there. Australia could only be reached by undertaking a journey of epic proportions! Captain Cook had landed there in 1770 – the first person to bring news of this exciting foreign land back to Europe. So, to shanty-singing sailors in the nineteenth century, Australia must still have held a mysterious and novel fascination.

South Australia is sung in strict four time, with strong emphasis on the first and third beats of each chorus line ("*Heave* away, *haul* away") as the sailors strained at their work. The tune is contained within a fairly limited range, except for the first note of each chorus, which is bellowed out an octave above the final note of the previous verse – creating a rousing, energising effect. It was, of course, sung on journeys between Britain and Australia. At the time, travelling from one to the other would have meant an arduous voyage across the Atlantic and around Cape Horn on the southern tip of South America, before striking out across the Pacific – two of the world's great oceans in one long journey (with a stop or two along the way, of course).

Being away from home for such a long period would be hard for anyone, and the sailors must have missed their families and friends. But there was something more important than that, of course: travelling to a new country was a chance to meet new girlfriends.

Australian girls here are represented by "Nancy Blair", a young woman who has a short-lived romance with a sailor before he has to leave her and travel back to other side of world.

This shanty was sung as ships departed, as the crew raised the anchor to leave the port. It captures all the excitements and hardships of travelling down under. With such long journey times, there were no certainties as to how long it would be before they made it home again.

BLOW THE MAN DOWN

As I was a-walking down Paradise Street
Way hey, blow the man down
A pretty young damsel I chanced for to meet
Give me some time to blow the man down!

I hailed her in English, she answered me clear
Way hey, blow the man down
"I'm from the Black Arrow bound to the
   Shakespeare"
Give me some time to blow the man down!

So I tailed her my flipper and took her in tow
Way hey, blow the man down
And yardarm to yardarm away we did go
Give me some time to blow the man down!

But as we were going she said unto me
Way hey, blow the man down
There's a spanking full-rigger just ready for sea
Give me some time to blow the man down!

That spanking full-rigger to New York was bound
Way hey, blow the man down
She was very well manned and very well found
Give me some time to blow the man down!

And as soon as that packet was out on the sea
Way hey, blow the man down
'Twas devilish hard treatment of every degree
Give me some time to blow the man down!

But as soon as that packet was clear of the bar
Way hey, blow the man down
The mate knocked me down with the end of
    a spar
Give me some time to blow the man down!

It's starboard and larboard on deck you will
    sprawl
Way hey, blow the man down
For Kicking Jack Williams commands the
    Black Ball
Give me some time to blow the man down!

So I give you fair warning before we belay
Way hey, blow the man down
Don't ever take heed of what pretty girls say
Give me some time to blow the man down!

There are lots of different versions of this well-known and very catchy shanty out there with differing lyrics, but the chorus is always the same. "Blow the man down" means "punch him to the ground" or "knock him down" – fittingly sung to a stumbling descending melody. Whichever variation of the words you know, one thing is certain: this is one of the more brutal shanties.

The version that I've chosen here tells the story of a sailor being roughed up on deck at the hands of his superiors. He meets a girl in Paradise Street, next to the Liverpool docks, who recommends a ship to him for his next voyage. He boards it for a voyage to New York, but ends up getting beaten relentlessly by the chief mate and captain. There were strict hierarchies on merchant ships, and "devilish hard treatment" was commonplace.

The sailor's first encounter with the girl is described using witty naval imagery. The pair are pictured as two ships drawing close alongside one another. "I tailed her my flipper" means "I gave her my hand", and the pair walk "yardarm to yardarm", meaning "shoulder to shoulder" (the yardarm was the horizontal spar across a ship's mast, where the sails hung from).

The ship the girl recommends turns out to be a dreadful choice, as the sailor suffers terribly at the hands of "Kicking Jack Williams". He was a real-life person – a notoriously harsh American captain on the New York–Liverpool shipping route. You'll find out

more about the "Black Ball" in the s[...]
Ball Line.

Like so many shanties, this song makes light o[...]
sailors' rough life. It seems it was all part and par[...]
the job at the time, and this song presumably helped
them take it all on the chin with a grim smile. I love the
rough and ready tune, which makes it fun and easy to
sing for all and sundry.

hanty The Black

of the

cel of

ıe day

ɹ the day
ɹexico

Chorus.
Oh! Heave heɹ ρ and away we'll go
Away Santianna
Heave her up and away we'll go
Along the plains of Mexico

Chorus

He gain'd the day at Molly-Del-Rey
Away Santianna
And General Taylor ran away
Along the plains of Mexico

Chorus

Oh Santiana fought for fame
Away Santianna
And Santianna gained a name
Along the plains of Mexico

Chorus

Santianna's men were true and brave
Away Santianna
Many found a hero's grave
Along the plains of Mexico

Chorus

Santianna was a damn fine man
Away Santianna
Till he ran afoul of Uncle Sam
Along the plains of Mexico

Chorus

Oh Santianna's day is o'er
Away Santianna
Santianna will fight no more
Along the plains of Mexico

Chorus

Now Santianna shovels gold
Away Santianna
Around Cape Horn in the ice and cold
Along the plains of Mexico

Chorus

We'll dig his grave with a silver spade
Away Santianna
And mark the spot where he was laid
Along the plains of Mexico

Chorus

For a change, here's a shanty that doesn't focus on sailors' lives. It's a song about history, war and politics, rather than women, drink and hardship. Part of what makes shanties so interesting is what they reveal about events around the world and how ordinary people saw them. Sailors travelled all around the world long before the general population could, and shanties like this one popularised historical figures across the globe and wrote historical events into legend.

"Santianna" is the Mexican general Antonio López de Santa Anna, who fought in the US–Mexico conflict between 1846 and 1848. His great opponent was the US major general Zachary Taylor, who later became president.

The war was closely fought, and the shanty celebrates the Mexican general's victories, although in reality Mexico lost the war. What's clear here is that whoever came up with the song was firmly on Mexico's side. A probable explanation for this is that *Santianna* was originally a song sung by slaves, who would have supported the enemies of their cruel American masters.

The syncopated rhythm at the beginning of each chorus lends this shanty real verve and vitality. There's a brilliant cover online by the shanty group *The Longest Johns* – it's well worth a listen.

HAUL AWAY, JOE

When I was just a little lad or so me mammy
    told me
Away, haul away, we'll haul away Joe
That if I didn't kiss the girls me lips would grow
    a-mouldy
Away, haul away, we'll haul away Joe

Chorus:
Away *Ho!* Haul away! We'll haul away together
Away, haul away, we'll haul away Joe
Away *Ho!* Haul away! We'll haul for better
    weather
Away, haul away, we'll haul away Joe

I used to have an Irish girl, but she got fat
    and lazy
Away, haul away, we'll haul away Joe
But now I've got a Bristol girl, and she just
    drives me crazy
Away, haul away, we'll haul away Joe

Chorus

Old Louis was the king of France before the
    revolution
Away, haul away, we'll haul away Joe
But then he got his head chopped off an' it
    spoiled his constitution.
Away, haul away, we'll haul away Joe

Chorus

You call yourself a second mate, you cannot tie
    a bowline
Away, haul away, we'll haul away Joe
You can't even stand up straight, when the
    packet she's a-rolling
Away, haul away, we'll haul away Joe

Chorus

Well now can't you see the black clouds
    a-gathering
Away, haul away, we'll haul away Joe
Well now can't you see the storm clouds
    a-rising
Away, haul away, we'll haul away Joe

Chorus

Shanties tend to be about all sorts of things that were important to sailors – from women to the weather, from mocking their commanding officers to disrespecting the French. Verse four aims particular scorn at the second mate, a subordinate officer on board ship. He was responsible for keeping discipline among the common crew, but he wasn't afforded the same seniority as the captain and chief mate, and still had to do a lot of the dirty work on deck. That made him an easy target – he wanted to be seen as one of the top dogs, but the crew would never grant him such an honour.

This is an example of a short-drag shanty – sung during tasks that required a short burst of energy. For instance, when the direction of the sails needed changing, the sailors sang *Haul Away, Joe* as they gave the ropes a series of sharp, powerful tugs. With its steady tempo and strong emphasis on the final syllable of each chorus line, this was the perfect shanty for short, concentrated jobs out on deck.

DERBY RAM

As I was going to Derby, 'twas on a market day
I met the finest ram, sirs, that ever was fed
    upon hay

Chorus:
That's a lie, that's a lie!
That's a lie, a lie, a lie!

This ram and I got drunk, sir, as drunk as drunk
    could be
And when we sobered up, sir, we were far away
    out on the sea

Chorus

This wonderful old ram, sir, was playful as a kid
He swallowed the captain's spyglass along with
    the bo'sun's fid

Chorus

One morning on the poop, sir, afore eight bells
    was struck
He climbed up to the sky's l yard and sat down
    on the truck

Chorus

This wonderful old ram, sir, he tried a silly trick
He tried to jump a five-barred fence and landed
    in a rick

Chorus

This wonderful old ram, sir, it grew two horns
    of brass
One grew out of his shoulder blade, t'other
    turned into a mast

Chorus

An' when this ram was killed, sir, the butcher
    was covered in blood
Five and twenty butcher boys were carried
    away by the flood

Chorus

And when this ram was dead, sir, they buried it
    in St. Joan's
It took ten men and an elephant to carry one of
    its bones

Chorus

The somewhat ridiculous nature of this shanty was adapted from a traditional folk song sung on land in Britain. It tells a nonsense story about a giant ram that ends up out at sea with a crew of sailors. A fantastical tale like this would lift any crew's spirits in a dull moment, and the shantyman would make up silly verses on the spot to entertain them even more.

The story of the Derby Ram originates from an ancient folk custom in the Midlands of England. In midwinter, a local man would dress up as a ram – with a sort of hobby horse costume made of sackcloth, topped by a goat's horned head. Dubbed "Old Tup", the man in ram costume would travel the nearby villages among a group of singing and dancing locals. They would stop at houses and knock on their front doors to ask for money, before enacting the ram's ritual slaughter. The Derby Ram was associated with fertility and good luck for the year, so locals usually handed over some money when it appeared at their door.

The song became so popular that it spread to America, where it was sung on land as well as at sea. Even George Washington supposedly knew it!

JOHNNY BOKER

Oh! Do, my Johnny Boker
Come rock and roll me over
Do! My Johnny Boker, do!

Oh! Do, my Johnny Boker
The skipper is a rover
Do! My Johnny Boker, do!

Oh! Do, my Johnny Boker
The mate he's never sober
Do! My Johnny Boker, do!

Oh! Do, my Johnny Boker
The bo'sun is a tailor
Do! My Johnny Boker, do!

Oh! Do, my Johnny Boker
We'll all go on a jamboree
Do! My Johnny Boker, do!

Oh! Do, my Johnny Boker
The packet is a rolling
Do! My Johnny Boker, do!

Oh! Do, my Johnny Boker
We'll pull and haul together
Do! My Johnny Boker, do!

Johnny Boker is a "sweating-up chant" – that is, a shanty sung while the sailors tightened the sails. They sang as they pulled the sails to maximum tautness with a few final, exhausting tugs on the ropes. All hands were needed on deck for this heavy-duty task, requiring a powerful burst of strength and effort. The sailors gave one big yank at the ropes at the end of each chorus line – either on the final word ("Do, my Johnny Boker, *do*!) or on an unpitched grunt just after the final word ("Do, my Johnny Boker, do – *huh!*"). The chorus was sung on an ascending scale, with the upward momentum of the music concentrating all the sailors' efforts on the final note.

In the first verse, "Rock and roll me over" is a reference to the back-and-forth motion of tugging the sails taut. Curiously enough, this is the origin of the term "rock and roll" as we know it today! The back-and-forth and side-to-side movements associated with original rock and roll dance patterns were really just a mundane practicality for sailors in the nineteenth century. Who knew?

OLD BILLY RILEY

Old Billy Riley was a dancing master
Old Billy Riley, oh, old Billy Riley!
Old Billy Riley's master of a drogher
Old Billy Riley, oh, old Billy Riley!

Master of a drogher bound for Antigua
Old Billy Riley, oh, old Billy Riley!
Old Billy Riley has a nice young daughter
Old Billy Riley, oh, old Billy Riley!

Oh, Missy Riley, little Missy Riley
Old Billy Riley, oh, old Billy Riley!
Had a pretty daughter, but we can't get at her
Old Billy Riley, oh, old Billy Riley!

Screw her up and away we go, boys
Old Billy Riley, oh, old Billy Riley!
One more pull and then belay, boys
Old Billy Riley, oh, old Billy Riley!

Originally a slave song sung on cotton-trading boats in the US, *Old Billy Riley* soon became popular as a sea shanty too. Why? Because it offered an opportunity to have a dig at the captain, of course.

Billy Riley, master of a drogher, could be an indirect reference to any ship's captain. Here he's sneeringly described as a "dancing master", which tells you all you need to know about sailors' attitudes to their commanding officers – implying the captain is a poser and a prancer in his fancy uniform. Singing about Billy Riley's daughter was a demeaning way of getting under the captain's skin, without visibly stepping out of line.

The "drogher" that Billy Riley commands is a type of ship that transported cotton supplies around the Caribbean. Antigua, where this particular ship is bound, was an important cotton producer. When the crew sing "screw her up" in the final lines, this sounds like a derogatory jibe at the captain's daughter, but at the same time it is a perfectly innocent-sounding reference to the way cotton was stored in a ship's hold. It had to be "screwed up" and compressed in order to store as much as possible in as little space as possible.

So, like many shanties, this song operates on several levels at once: one perfectly proper, the other anything but.

THE BLACK BALL LINE

In the Black Ball line I served my time
To me way-aye-aye, hurray-ah
And that's the line where you can shine
Hurrah for the Black Ball Line

The Black Ball Ships are good and true
To me way-aye-aye, hurray-ah
They are the ships for me and you
Hurrah for the Black Ball Line

For once there was a Black Ball Ship
To me way-aye-aye, hurray-ah
That fourteen knots an hour could clip
Hurrah for the Black Ball Line

They'll carry you along through frost and snow
To me way-aye-aye, hurray-ah
And take you where the wind don't blow
Hurrah for the Black Ball Line

You will surely find a rich gold mine
To me way-aye-aye, hurray-ah
Just take a trip in the Black Ball Line
Hurrah for the Black Ball Line

Just take a trip to Liverpool
To me way-aye-aye, hurray-ah
To Liverpool, that Yankee school
Hurrah for the Black Ball Line

The Yankee sailors you'll see there
To me way-aye-aye, hurray-ah
With red-top boots and short-cut hair
Hurrah for the Black Ball Line

At Liverpool docks we bid adieu
To me way-aye-aye, hurray-ah
To Poll and Bet and lovely Sue
Hurrah for the Black Ball Line

And now we're bound for New York Town
To me way-aye-aye, hurray-ah
It's there we'll drink, and sorrow drown
Hurrah for the Black Ball Line

The Black Ball Line was a fleet of transatlantic transport ships (so-called "packet" ships) carrying cargo, mail, and passengers between Liverpool and New York City. Established in 1817, the Black Ball Line ushered in a new era of faster and cheaper transportation and travel to far-flung destinations—essentially a precursor to the age of the ocean liner.

The ships carried a black circular marking on the main sail as the company's distinctive logo.

The ships themselves were clippers, adapted to make journeys faster in order to meet increasing commercial demands in the early nineteenth century. They brought journey times between US and the UK down to four weeks – an impressively speedy trip back then! Sometimes they could even manage the return journey to the UK in three, if the winds were favourable.

There may have been plenty to cheer about on the Black Ball Line, but the ships were also notorious for the harsh discipline onboard at the hands of mercilessly exacting officers. So there may well have been an undercurrent of fear and resentment running through this shanty, despite its grand, march-like melody. Mostly, though, it's a celebration of the clippers' revolutionary speed and the exotic destinations they were capable of reaching in seemingly no time at all – before the aeroplane came along and put paid to that idea.

WELLERMAN

There once was a ship that put to sea
The name of the ship was the Billy of Tea
The winds blew up, her bow dipped down
Oh blow, my bully boys, blow

Chorus:
Soon may the Wellerman come
To bring us sugar and tea and rum
One day, when the tonguing is done
We'll take our leave and go

She'd not been two weeks from shore
When down on her a right whale bore
The captain called all hands and swore
He'd take that whale in tow

Chorus

Before the boat had hit the water
The whale's tail came up and caught her
All hands to the side, harpooned and fought her
When she dived down low

Chorus

No line was cut, no whale was freed
The captain's mind was not of greed
And he belonged to the Whaleman's creed
She took that ship in tow

Chorus

For forty days or even more
The line went slack then tight once more
All boats were lost, there were only four
But still that whale did go

Chorus

As far as I've heard, the fight's still on
The line's not cut, and the whale's not gone
The Wellerman makes his regular call
To encourage the captain, crew and all

Chorus

A song that needs no introduction – it's the one that changed my life. It's a fan favourite for its thumping beat and catchy tune, and it's absolutely begging for people to join in with the melody or add harmonies of their own. The best feeling as a singer is knowing that people are enjoying a song while you perform it, and that's the feeling I get every time I sing *Wellerman*.

But what on earth is a "Wellerman"? Who are "bully boys"? And is "tonguing" as naughty as it sounds?

Let's start with a bit of background. This shanty originated in New Zealand, and it tells the story of a ship hunting for whales. The whaling industry was booming in the nineteenth century, because there was a lucrative trade in whale oil, which could be used as an industrial lubricant or as lamp fuel.

There was a whaling station in Otakou Harbour, New Zealand, founded by the Weller brothers, who were merchant traders. At the whaling station, workers would cut up the whales that the ships had brought in. It's possible that *Wellerman* was a "cutting-in shanty" that the workers sang as they did this. In the chorus, "tonguing" might refer to the process of cutting blubber into strips to be made into whale oil – or it might just mean cutting out the whale's tongue, which was apparently its most edible part.

As for the "Wellerman", he was one of the Weller brothers' employees, who would arrive by ship to pay the whaling station workers. They were paid not in money, but in clothing, spirits and tobacco. So the "sugar and tea and rum" they look forward to in the chorus is effectively their wages. "Bully boys" is a phrase you'll see in a lot of shanties – referring to the rough and ready crew.

Obviously, whales are big beasts. And hunting them was especially difficult in the days before mechanisation. No matter how strong and skilled a crew was, there were big risks involved. The verses of *Wellerman* tell the story of a whale hunt that sinks several ships – and the song ends by telling us with a wry smile that the struggle's probably still going.

Whaling off the coast of New Zealand was eventually banned in 1965, so this song might have died out, had it not been recorded by the folk song collector Neil Colquhoun. Thank goodness he did! It differs from the other songs in this book in that it's really more of a

ballad than a shanty – it's more about the story, and less about keeping people in time as they work.

Part of what's made *Wellerman* so popular, I think, is its pure simplicity and the crystal clarity of its tune. There are no big challenges involved in singing it, no riffs or difficult high notes to pull off. It's a song that everyone can sing and bang along to together, no matter how much of a musician you are. It'll get stuck in your head and just go round and round and round. And that's the beauty of it.

Without *Wellerman*, my life would have been completely different. I owe a lot of thanks to this shanty.

ROLLING DOWN TO OLD MAUI

It's a damn tough life full of toil and strife
We whalermen undergo
And we won't give a damn when the gales are
    done
How hard the winds did blow
For we're homeward bound from the Arctic
    grounds
With a good ship taut and free
And we won't give a damn when we drink our
    rum
With the girls from old Maui

Chorus:
Rolling down to old Maui, me boys
Rolling down to old Maui
We're homeward bound from the Arctic grounds
Rolling down to old Maui

Once more we sail with the northerly gales
Through the ice and wind and rain
Them coconut fronds, them tropical shores
We soon shall see again
Six hellish months we've passed away
On the cold Kamchatka sea

But now we're bound from the Arctic grounds
Rolling down to old Maui

Chorus

Once more we sail with the Northerly gales
Towards our island home
Our whaling done, our mainmast sprung
And we ain't got far to roam
Our stuns'l's bones is carried away
What care we for that sound
A living gale is after us
Thank God we're homeward bound

Chorus

How soft the breeze through the island trees
Now the ice is far astern
Them native maids, them tropical glades
Is awaiting our return
Even now their big brown eyes look out
Hoping some fine day to see
Our baggy sails, running 'fore the gales
Rolling down to old Maui

Chorus

Much like *Wellerman*, *Rolling Down to Old Maui* is a whaling ballad, which was mostly sung during sailors' rest time (so strictly speaking, it's a forebitter rather than a shanty). Singing was not just for work – it was also a fun way to pass the time out at sea, especially given how few other forms of entertainment were available.

Maui is the second largest island in Hawaii, and this song first emerged hundreds of miles north of the islands, in the seas between the eastern tip of Russia and the western tip of Alaska. Whaling crews left the warmth of Hawaii behind to hunt in those icy waters, and as the crew awaited their return from whaling,

shivering in the wintry cold, they sang this rousing song, picturing the women who would welcome them back to Maui and the rum that would be waiting for them there to warm them up again.

This ballad is more explicit in its complaints about life at sea than most shanties, and the minor key lends the verses an air of lamentation. But the song modulates into the major for the first line of the chorus, before returning to the minor – painting a touching picture of hope mingled with suffering, as the sailors long for the cosy and comforting climate of Hawaii after six months away in the brutal cold and damp. There would have been nothing more heartening than the idea of waking up in a few weeks' time with a hangover, beneath the sun's dazzling rays.

BLOOD RED ROSES

Oh me boots and clothes are all in pawn
Go down, you blood red roses, go down
And it's bloody draughty 'round Cape Horn
Go down, you blood red roses, go down

Chorus:
Oh, you pinks and posies
Go down, you blood red roses, go down

But it's 'round Cape Horn we all must go
Go down, you blood red roses, go down
For that is where the whale-fish blow
Go down, you blood red roses, go down

Chorus

My dear old mother wrote to me
Go down, you blood red roses, go down
Ah son, won't you come home from sea
Go down, you blood red roses, go down

Chorus

It's 'round the Cape that we must go
Go down, you blood red roses, go down
Though we be beaten with rain and snow
Go down, you blood red roses, go down

Chorus

It's growl you may, but go you must
Go down, you blood red roses, go down
You growl too loud, your head they'll bust
Go down, you blood red roses, go down

Chorus

Just one more pull and that will do
Go down, you blood red roses, go down
For we're the boys to pull her through
Go down, you blood red roses, go down

Chorus

There are many different theories about the lyrics to this enigmatic shanty. It's unclear who or what "red roses" are a reference to, but what we do know is that this was a halyard shanty sung aboard whaling boats – and the shantyman has to be in good voice to sing it, bellowing out the last word of each line on a sustained note at the top of his range.

The red roses might represent the women back home, waiting for months on end for their sailors to return. Alternatively, they might be a reference to British naval officers in their red coats. The most poetic (and the grisliest) theory, though, is that the chorus is about a long and bloody whale hunt.

Sailors didn't necessarily enjoy their work, and hunting whales was a particularly arduous task. Even when sailors hit the target with the harpoon, these big beasts could keep swimming for hours – towing the boat for miles on end – before the wound actually killed them.

The theory goes that if a whale was hit in the lungs by a sailor's harpoon, it would emit a red rose-shaped mist from its blowhole when it came to the surface to breathe. So the line "Go down, you blood red roses" could be an expression of grim awe at the sight, and of angst at having to witness the whale in its death throes. In this scenario, "go down" presumably means "hurry up and die". It would have been gruelling to watch – and harder work still to tow the creature back in once it was dead.

Like any job, being a sailor wasn't all roses.

RANDY-DANDY-O

Now we are ready to head for the Horn
Way, ay, roll and go!
Our boots and our clothes boys are all in the
pawn
To me rollicking randy-dandy-o!

Chorus:
Heave a pawl, oh, heave away
Way, ay, roll and go!
The anchor's on board and the cable's all stored
To me rollicking randy-dandy-o!

Soon we'll be warping her out through the
locks
Way, ay, roll and go!
Where the pretty young gals all come down in
their flocks
To me rollicking randy-dandy-o!

Chorus

Come breast the bars, bullies, and heave her away
Way, ay, roll and go!
Soon we'll be rolling her 'way down the bay
To me rollicking randy-dandy-o!

Sing goodbye to Sally and goodbye to Sue
Way, ay, roll and go!
For we are the boyos who can kick 'er through
To me rollicking randy-dandy-o!

Chorus

Oh, man the stout capstan and heave with a will
Way, ay, roll and go!
Soon we'll be driving her 'way down the hill
To me rollicking randy-dandy-o!

Chorus

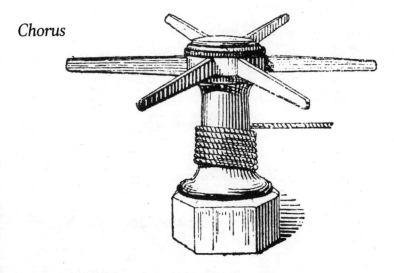

Heave away, bullies, ye parish-rigged bums
Way, ay, roll and go!
Take your hands from your pockets and don't
    suck your thumbs
To me rollicking randy-dandy-o!

Chorus

Roust 'er up, bullies, the wind's drawing free
Way, ay, roll and go!
Let's get the glad-rags on and drive 'er to sea
To me rollicking randy-dandy-o!

Chorus

We're outward bound for Vallipo Bay
Way, ay, roll and go!
Get cracking, my lads, 'tis a hell of a way!
To me rollicking randy-dandy-o!

Chorus

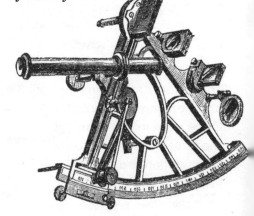

This shanty has amazing energy to it, and the chorus's descending melody and thumping beat really captures the sound of sailors hard at work under the blaze of the sun. The lyrics detail all the final preparations a crew had to make for their ship's next voyage. They got all the equipment ready and sang farewell to their loved ones, before setting out from the harbour on another long journey. "Roll and go" is naval slang for "sail away".

As for "Randy-Dandy", this is possibly a sarcastic reference to the ship's commanding officers. Most sailors probably thought of the uniformed officers as dandies, who constantly felt the need to give the sailors a "rollicking" (a telling off) simply to assert their authority. The lack of respect for the officers is even clearer from the crew's description as "parish-rigged bums" – meaning that the ship they're working on is very poorly equipped.

The sailors are heading out on another long journey around Cape Horn in this shanty, so the final destination could be anywhere from San Francisco to Sydney.

Before arriving, the ship will stop off at "Vallipo Bay" – that's Valparaíso, on the west coast of Chile, which was a popular stopping point for ships after rounding Cape Horn. Whether it's the US or Australia they're ultimately heading for, the last line of the song is true enough: it really is a hell of a way!

THE MAID OF AMSTERDAM

In Amsterdam there lived a maid
Mark well what I do say!
In Amsterdam there lived a maid
And she was mistress of her trade

Chorus:
I'll go no more a-roving with you fair maid!
A-roving, a-roving
Since roving's been my ru-i-in
I'll go no more a roving with you fair maid!

I asked this maid to take a walk
Mark well what I do say!
I asked this maid out for a walk
That we might have some private talk

Chorus

Then a great big Dutchman rammed my bow
Mark well what I do say!
For a great big Dutchman rammed my bow
And said, "Young man, dees ees mein frau!"

Chorus
Then take fair warning boys from me,
Mark well what I do say!
So take fair warning boys from me
With other men's wives, don't make too free
I'll go no more a roving with you fair maid!

Chorus

It's fair to say that this is one of the bawdier shanties. In most versions that were actually sung out at sea, the shantyman's filthy tongue would probably have rendered it unprintable.

It tells the story of a brief encounter between a sailor and a young woman in Amsterdam. In some versions she makes the first move, and in others he does. Either way, *The Maid of Amsterdam* usually serves as a cautionary tale of some sort – about the perils of picking up married women, or of spending all your wages on prostitutes.

This is a classic shanty tune in sprightly four-time, with a skipping, carefree rhythm that perfectly captures the sailor's laissez-faire attitude to "roving" and romance.

PADDY DOYLE'S BOOTS

To me way-ay-ay yah!
We'll pay Paddy Doyle for his boots!

To me way-ay-ay yah!
We'll all drink whiskey and gin!

To me way-ay-ay yah!
We'll all shave under the chin!

To me way-ay-ay yah!
We'll all throw mud at the cook!

To me way-ay-ay yah!
The dirty old man's on the poop!

To me way-ay-ay yah!
We'll bouse her up and be done!

To me way-ay-ay yah!
We'll pay Paddy Doyle for his boots!

Paddy Doyle's Boots is a "bunt" shanty – a song that sailors sang while lashing the rolled-up sail (the "bunt") to the horizontal beam from which it hung (the "yardarm"). They had to climb up rigging to reach the yardarm high up on the mast, before lifting the sail onto it and securing it. It wasn't a long task, but it was one that required a good deal of strength. That's why this is such a short shanty – but a very important one. It is possible that the whole shanty was sung in unison, but this remains disputed. In any case, the tune twists and turns, with a strong sense of camaraderie and a touch of mischief about it.

It's uncertain who exactly Paddy Doyle was, and why seamen were after his boots. One theory is that he was a Liverpool cobbler who provided sailors with suitable footwear for their next voyage. Alternatively, the name might be a reference to boarding house masters in port towns. When they arrived at their destination, sailors would often stay in these boarding houses before setting out to sea again, and they would buy equipment for their next trip from the owner of the boarding house. So perhaps this is what's meant by "paying Paddy Doyle for his boots".

Knowing sailors' humour, though, it might just be a joke about nicking a pair of boots when the boarding house master isn't looking!

LIZA LEE

O the smartest clipper you can find
A-ho, way-ho, are you almost done
Is the Margaret Evans of the Blue Cross Line
So clear the track let the bullgine run

Chorus:
To me hey rig-a-jig in a low-backed car
A-ho, way-ho, are you almost done
With Liza Lee all on my knee
So clear the track let the bullgine run

O the Margaret Evans of the Blue Cross Line
A-ho, way-ho, are you almost done
She's never a day behind her time
So clear the track let the bullgine run

Chorus

O we're outward bound for New York Town
A-ho, way-ho, are you almost done
Them bowery gals we'll waltz around
So clear the track let the bullgine run

Chorus

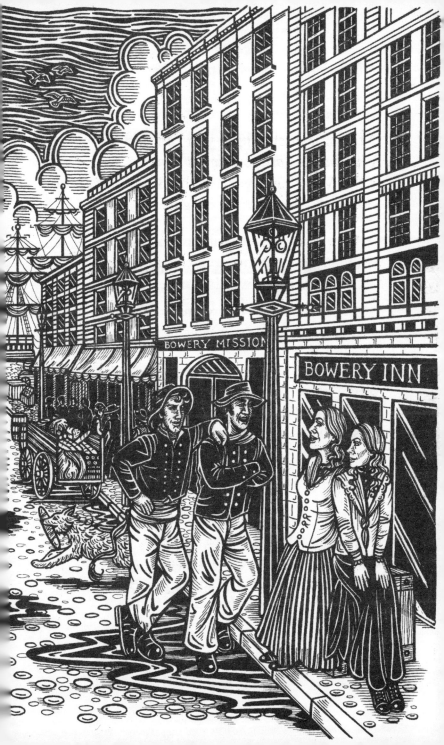

When we've stowed our freight at the West
    Street Pier
A-ho, way-ho, are you almost done
It's home to Liverpool then we'll steer
So clear the track let the bullgine run

Chorus

O them bowery gals will give us fun
A-ho, way-ho, are you almost done
Chatham Street dives is home from home
So clear the track let the bullgine run

Chorus

When we all get back to Liverpool town
A-ho, way-ho, are you almost done
I'll stand ye whiskeys all around
So clear the track let the bullgine run

Chorus

O heave a pawl O bear a hand
A-ho, way-ho, are you almost done
Just one more pull and make her stand
So clear the track let the bullgine run

Chorus

O Liza Lee, will you be mine?
A-ho, way-ho, are you almost done
I'll dress you up in silk so fine
So clear the track let the bullgine run

Chorus

And when I'm home again from sea
A-ho, way-ho, are you almost done
Oh Liza, you shall marry me
So clear the track let the bullgine run

Chorus

I'll stay with you upon the shore
A-ho, way-ho, are you almost done
And back to sea will go no more
So clear the track let the bullgine run

Chorus

This shanty has a cheerful beat and gruff, impatient choruses that make it a lot of fun to sing. The nonsense lines ("hey rig-a-jig") lend a rawness and spontaneity to the song, in which a sailor looks forward to marrying his sweetheart when he returns home. The "bullgine" is slang for a railway engine, so "Let the bullgine run"

119

suggests the sailor's impatience to strike out for home and get back as quickly as possible.

In the meantime, though, there's a day or two for him to enjoy in New York before the ship sets off home again! The "bowery girls" in the song are a reference to a street on Manhattan called Bowery. There's clearly plenty of excitement to be found before the crew re-boards for the return journey.

The Margaret Evans (verse 1) was a ship that travelled between New York and British ports. It was a "packet ship" that carried mail, cargo and passengers back and forth between the two.

This shanty has its roots in a mixture of Irish and African-American influences. It's fast-moving, optimistic, and is a lot of fun to listen and sing along to.

BULLY IN THE ALLEY

Chorus:
Oh, help me Bob, I'm bully in the alley
Way hey, bully in the alley
Help me Bob, I'm bully in the alley
Bully down in Shinbone Al

Now Sally is a girl in Shinbone Alley
Way hey, bully in the alley
Sally is the girl that I spliced nearly
Bully down in Shinbone Al

Chorus

For seven long years I courted little Sally
Way hey, bully in the alley
But all she did was dilly and dally
Bully down in Shinbone Al

Chorus

If I ever get back, I'll marry little Sally
Way hey, bully in the alley
Have six kids and live in Shinbone Alley
Bully down in Shinbone Al

Chorus

Picture the scene. Your ship has docked in a foreign port to unload its cargo, and you've got a precious few hours on land before you head out to sea again.

You step ashore – it's evening, the sun is setting over the sparkling sea, and lanterns are being lit across

the town as night descends. You've never been to this place before and you've only got one evening here to make the most of. What do you and your crewmates do?

You do what all sensible sailors with an evening on land would do. You head straight to the pub.

Bully in the Alley is a shanty about the state you find yourself in a few hours later, when you've had more than a few too many. In nautical slang, "bully" means drunk. So the chorus – "Help me Bob, I'm bully in the alley" – roughly translates as, "Someone give me a hand, I'm wasted!"

As you can imagine, some sailors could hold their drink better than others. So if one of them got horribly drunk, as in this song, his mates would find somewhere safe to leave him – and an alley was a good bet. "Shinbone Alley" is a street name that pops up in several Caribbean port towns, so it's likely this shanty originated on ships that travelled to North America.

And what about "Bob"? Well, "help me, Bob" is an archaic Scots saying to express surprise – the kind of surprise you feel when you suddenly find you can't stand up. But in this shanty, it sounds like Bob is also that crewmate who's always there for you when you're not feeling a hundred percent.

Coming ashore was a rare chance for a ship's crew to cut loose and have a good time, and the verses tell the story of a sailor's onshore antics courting a young woman (presumably between pub trips).

I first came across this shanty on YouTube, where it's sung by the shanty group Kimber's Men, with the bass John Bromley as soloist. Check it out – his booming voice blew me away.

You don't have to have sailed the high seas to relate to a shanty like this one. We've all been there.

DON'T FORGET YOUR OLD SHIPMATE

Safe and sound at home again, let the waters
  roar, Jack
Safe and sound at home again, let the waters
  roar, Jack

Chorus:
*Long we've tossed on the rolling main, now we're
  safe ashore, Jack*
*Don't forget yer old shipmate, faldee-raldee-raldee-
  raldee rye-eye-doe!*

Since we sailed from Plymouth Sound, four
  years gone, or nigh, Jack
Was there ever chummies, now, such as you
  and I, Jack?

Chorus

We have worked the self-same gun,
  quarterdeck division
Sponger I and loader you, through the whole
  commission

Chorus

Oftentimes have we laid out, toil nor danger
    fearing
Tugging out the flapping sail to the weather
    earing

Chorus

When the middle watch was on, and the time
    went slow, boy
Who could choose a rousing stave, who like
    Jack or Joe, boy?

Chorus

There she swings, an empty hulk, not a soul
 below now
Number seven starboard mess misses Jack and
 Joe now

Chorus

But the best of friends must part, fair or foul
 the weather
Hand yer flipper for a shake, now a drink
 together

Chorus

Sticklers will say this isn't strictly a shanty, but
it's too much of a classic sea song not to include!
It was originally a Royal Navy song dating back
to the Napoleonic era (so before shanties were
mainstream). It was popularised in the film *Master
and Commander*, and it's still sung in the Navy today,
to the same jaunty tune.

Don't Forget Your Old Shipmate is a song of
comradeship between fellow sailors, which endures
even after returning home and coming ashore. The
sailors have spent long months out at sea together,
working on the gundeck of a warship. One is a
"sponger", who would clean the cannon to get rid of
any sparks or dirt, and the other is a "loader", who

would then load the cannon with fresh gunpowder to attack the enemy. Even in their hours off duty, this pair of sailors are in the same "mess" (the area where the crew ate, with separate messes designated for crew members of different ranks).

Parting ways with a shipmate at the end of a long voyage, after living together in cramped conditions for so long, must have been strange and surreal. But a song like this would have kept the memory of all your old shipmates alive for a long time to come.

STRIKE THE BELL

Up on the poop deck, walking all about
There stands the second mate, so sturdy and so
  stout
What he is a-thinking, he don't know himself
And we wish that he would hurry up and strike,
  strike the bell

Chorus:
Strike the bell, second mate, and let us go below
Look well to windward, you can see it's going to
  blow
Looking at the glass, you can see that it fell
And we wish that you would hurry up and strike,
  strike the bell

Down on the main deck, working on the pumps
Is the poor larboard watch wishing for their
  bunks
Looking out to windward you can see a mighty
  swell
And we wish that you would hurry up and
  strike, strike the bell

Chorus

Down in the wheelhouse, old Anderson stands
Grasping at the helm with his frostbitten hands
Looking cockeyed at the compass, but the
    course is clear as... well...
And we wish that you would hurry up and
    strike, strike the bell

Chorus

Well, down in his cabin our gallant captain
    stands
Looking out the transom with
    a spyglass in his hands
What he is a-thinking, we all
    know very well
He's thinking more to shorten
    ail, then striking the bell

Chorus

Strike the Bell is one of the most relatable shanties out there. It's about checking the time at work to find out how long there is to go until your shift ends.

The sailors' working day was organised in four-hour shifts, with four hours on duty followed by four hours' rest. During the rest period, sailors would "go below", leaving the main deck and going down to their quarters.

During each shift, the second mate rang a bell every half hour to keep time. (To find out more about the second mate, see *Haul Away, Joe*.) The bell bonged once half an hour into the shift, twice after an hour, three times after an hour and a half, and so on – until eight chimes signalled the end of the shift. So the sailors always knew how much longer they had until their next break, which they would have anticipated eagerly. Their work out on the main deck was cold, wet and exhausting, and each strike of the bell brought them that little bit closer to some much-needed respite.

All this is reflected in the shanty's cheerful melody and energetic tempo, as the sailors goad the second mate into ringing the bell. Singing this shanty helped to make the time pass a little more quickly, as they looked forward to resting up, warming up and drying out.

FIRE DOWN BELOW

Fire in the galley, fire in the house
Fire down below
Fire in the beef kid, scorching the scouse
Fire down below boys, fire down below

Fire in the forepeak, fire in the main
Fire down below
Fire in the windlass, fire in the chain
Fire down below boys, fire down below

Fire in the lifeboat, fire in the gig
Fire down below
Fire in the pigsty, roasting the pig
Fire down below boys, fire down below

Fire on the orlop, fire in the hold
Fire down below
Fire in the strong room, melting the gold
Fire down below boys, fire down below

Fire round the capstan, fire on the mast
Fire down below
Fire on the main deck, burning it fast
Fire down below boys, fire down below

Fire in the cabin, fire burning wood
Fire down below
Fire in the store room spoiling all the food
Fire down below boys, fire down below

Fire in the keg, fire everywhere we go
Fire down below
Fire in the galley, the cook didn't know
Fire down below boys, fire down below

Fire on the waters, fire high above
Fire down below
Fire in our hearts for the friends that we love
Fire down below boys, fire down below

Sailors sang this "pump" shanty while bailing water out of the ship. Sea spray and rainwater drained into the hold from above, or seeped in through cracks in the hull, and it had to be pumped out again for safety's sake. This was a less arduous task than heaving bars around the capstan or hauling ropes, but it was extremely monotonous. Needless to say, this perky tune made the best of a boring situation.

Pumping all the water out of the hold took a long time, so there are lots of verses to this shanty – far more than can be written down all in one place. *Fire Down Below* was the perfect opportunity for any shantyman who wanted to get creative on the spot.

There was a very real risk of fire back when ships were still made of wood. So the lyrics reflected a genuine fear on deck. If a fire started out at sea, there was nowhere to hide and no way to escape. Hence the dark and ominous tune to a thumping, threatening beat.

But fire "down below" perhaps implies something even more gruesome. Sailors had a bit of a reputation when they came ashore, and sailors with wages to spend after months of cooped-up tedium often headed to brothels. This brought with it a high risk of contracting syphilis – leading to burning pains "down below". No bucket of water was likely to put that particular fire out any time soon.

ONE MORE DAY

Chorus:
Only one more day, me Johnny
One more day
Oh, rock 'n' roll me over
One more day

Oh, have you heard the news, me Johnny
One more day
We're homeward bound tomorrow
One more day

Chorus

Don't you hear the old man growling
One more day
Don't you hear the mate a-howling
One more day
Don't you hear the capstan pawling
One more day
Don't you hear the pilot bawling
One more day

Chorus

Only one more day a-howling
One more day
Can't you hear the gals a-calling
One more day
Only one more day a-furling
One more day
Only one more day a-cursing
One more day

Chorus

Oh, heave and sight the anchor, Johnny
One more day
For we're close aboard the port, Johnny
One more day
Only one more day for Johnny
One more day
And your pay-day's nearly due, Johnny
One more day

Chorus

Then put out your long-tail blue, Johnny
One more day
Make your port and take your pay, Johnny
One more day
Only one more day a-pumping, Johnny
One more day
Only one more day a-bracing, Johnny
One more day

Chorus

Oh, we're homeward bound today, Johnny
One more day
We'll leave her without sorrow, Johnny
One more day
Pack your bags today me Johnny
One more day
Oh, and leave her where she lies, Johnny
One more day

Chorus

Only one more day a-working, Johnny
One more day
Oh, come rock 'n' roll me over
One more day
No more gales or heavy weather
One more day
Only one more day together
One more day

Chorus

Like *Fire Down Below*, *One More Day* is a pump shanty, in which the crew look forward to their imminent arrival back home. It captures that warm, joyful feeling you get when your favourite place finally appears in the distance following a long and arduous journey. After being tossed about on the rough seas for months on end, nothing could beat the prospect of a night in your own bed.

This shanty had its roots in America, where it was supposedly first sung aboard riverboats. It soon caught on and spread from there onto the high seas. Seamen sang it shortly before coming into port, when the long-awaited end was in sight and home was near at hand.

One More Day gives a flavour of all aspects of sea life – the heavy work, the growling officers, the cry of the seabirds, the roll of the ship in rough seas – all mingled in one jubilant shanty with the simplest of choruses. Suddenly, all the things to look forward to when they come on shore are within touching distance – the girls waiting for them at home, a handful of wages to spend, and a period of respite from brutal storms and hard labour.

LEAVE HER, JOHNNY

Oh, the times are hard and the wages low
Leave Her Johnny, leave her
And the grub is bad and the gales do blow
Leave Her Johnny, leave her

Chorus:
Leave Her Johnny, leave her
Leave Her Johnny, leave her
For the voyage is long and the winds do blow
But it's time for us to leave her

I thought I heard the old captain say
Leave Her Johnny, leave her
You can go ashore and take your pay
Leave Her Johnny, leave her

Chorus

Oh, the wind was foul and the sea ran high
Leave Her Johnny, leave her
She shipped it green and none went by
Leave Her Johnny, leave her

Chorus

I hate to sail on this rotten tub
Leave Her Johnny, leave her
No grog allowed and rotten grub
Leave Her Johnny, leave her

Chorus

We swear by rote for want of more
Leave Her Johnny, leave her
Oh, now we're through so we'll go on shore
Leave Her Johnny, leave her

Chorus

This shanty means a lot to me. It's the first one I sang and posted online, and it carries one of the most beautiful tunes out there. In December 2020, the shanty group The Longest Johns released a video of hundreds of people singing this together online – it really embodies the sense of community and solidarity that shanties foster.

But like so many sea shanties, despite its moving melody, it shines a light on the less than beautiful realities of life at sea. *Leave Her, Johnny* is a "growling" shanty – one that gave a ship's crew an opportunity to vent their frustrations as they worked. The song complains about everything that can go wrong for a sailor on board ship – from food supplies going rotten over the course of the voyage, to the terrible pay, to the stormy weather and the threat it posed to the sailors' lives. Remember, losing a crew member in a storm was not a rare event 200 years ago.

With these brutal experiences in mind, the sailors ask the captain ("Johnny") to leave her (the ship) behind – and not put out to sea in such terrible conditions again. They simply don't want to have to endure it all again.

Leave Her, Johnny was sung at the end of a voyage, once the ship had docked: the crew would sing it as they pumped water from deck before going ashore.

Growling shanties gave the shantyman the chance to invent verses on the spot, complaining about specific problems that the crew had suffered on that particular trip. Every voyage was different, so the trials and tribulations faced on each journey differed too. The shantyman's improvisations would keep the sailors entertained and allow them to let off steam about their own personal hardships. Although the crew always sang the same line in response as they worked, they poured all their frustrations into those few words. Complaining directly to the officers on board ship

would most likely have been a punishable offence, so shanties provided their only opportunity to make their feelings audibly known.

Leave Her, Johnny features in the video game *Assassin's Creed*, so it always goes down well with people who recognise it from that. But there's so much more to this shanty than meets the eye. It tells you everything you need to know about the harsh reality of making a living at sea. Despite the extraordinary array of places they travelled to, there was always plenty to grumble about along the way.

POOR OLD HORSE

A poor old man came riding by
And we say so, and we know so
Oh, a poor old man came riding by
Oh, poor old man

Says I, "Old man, your horse will die"
And we say so, and we know so
And if he dies, we'll tan his hide
Oh, poor old man

And if he don't, I'll ride him again
And we say so, and we know so
And I'll ride him, till the Lord knows when
Oh, poor old man

Oh, he's dead as a nail in the lamp room door
And we say so, and we know so
And he won't come worrying us no more
Oh, poor old man

We'll use the hair of his tail to sew our sails
And we say so, and we know so
And the iron of his shoes to make deck nails
Oh, poor old man

The shanty here is a strange one. It was sung only once per voyage, to accompany a mysterious and peculiar ritual.

This quirky ceremony was all to do with money. When sailors embarked on a voyage, they received a month's pay in advance. They often left this money with their families, or they spent it on new equipment or entertainment prior to departure. Because they'd already received and spent their first month's pay on land, for that first month out at sea, it felt like they were working for free.

Once the first month of the voyage had passed, the sailors started "earning" again. So they had a ceremony to celebrate. Gathering up discarded bits and pieces on board – barrels, ropes, old bits of sail, and so on – they bundled them all together to concoct a makeshift horse. They then paraded the horse around the deck while singing this morose melody, before hoisting it up into the air on a rope and dropping it into the sea.

The ritual was known as "paying off the dead horse" – a way of waving goodbye to that arduous first month, when it felt like they were slogging away with no reward.

THE FISHES' LAMENTATION

As we were a-fishing off Happisburgh light
Shooting and hauling and trawling all night

Chorus:
In the windy old weather, stormy old weather
When the wind blows we all pull together
Blow ye winds westerly, blow ye winds, blow
Jolly sou'wester, boys, steady she goes

Then up jumped a herring, the queen of the sea
Says "Now, old skipper, you cannot catch me"

Chorus

We sighted a thresher a-slashing his tail
"Time now, old skipper, to hoist up your sail"

Chorus

Then along comes a mackerel with strips on his
   back
"Time now, old skipper, to shift your main tack"

Chorus

And up jumps a Slipsole as strong as a horse
Says "Now, old skipper, you're miles off course"

Chorus

Then along comes plaice who's got spots on
   his side
Says "Not much longer these seas you can ride"

Chorus

Then up rears a conger as long as a mile
"Winds coming east'ly," he says with a smile

Chorus

"I think what these fishes are saying is right
We'll haul up our gear now and steer for the
   light"

Chorus

The magical and mysterious folklore of the sea is in full swing here. This shanty tells the story of an array of fish leaping out of the sea to give the captain directions, and to warn the crew of an impending storm.

It has its origins in Britain: the boat in the story is sailing off the coast of Norfolk in the east of England, within sight of the iconic Happisburgh lighthouse. The song was sometimes sung as a "forebitter" – that is, a tune that sailors sang off-duty to keep themselves entertained, rather than a working song to keep themselves in time with one another. But sometimes it was also used as a capstan shanty for heaving tasks. It's the perfect song for both scenarios. There was endless scope for improvisation and entertainment here: the leader of the singing could simply keep adding new fish each verse until his crewmates could no longer contain their laughter – or to keep them chuckling until the job was done. Further verses to this shanty make mention of sharks, whale, codfish, eels, lobsters...

ROLL THE WOODPILE DOWN

A-way down South where the cocks do crow!
  Hey!
Way down in Florida
Them girls all dance to the old banjo
And we'll roll the woodpile down

Chorus:
Rollin'! *Rollin'!* Rollin'! *Rollin'!*
Rollin' the whole world round!
That fine gal'a mine's on the Georgia line!
And we'll roll the woodpile down!

Oh, what can you do in Tampa Bay? *Hey!*
Way down in Florida
But give them pretty girls all your pay
And we'll roll the woodpile down

Chorus

We'll roll 'em high and we'll roll 'em low! *Hey!*
Way down in Florida
We'll roll 'er up and away we'll go!
And we'll roll the woodpile down

Chorus

Oh roust and bust her is the cry! *Hey!*
Way down in Florida
A sailor's wage is never high
And we'll roll the woodpile down

Chorus

Oh, one more pull and that will do! *Hey!*
Way down in Florida
For we're the boys to kick her through!
And we'll roll the woodpile down

This shanty began life as a slave song. Slaves in the US sang it aboard riverboats transporting lumber southwards from Georgia to Florida – which explains how a pile of wood became the star of the song. "Roll" simply means "sail" or "row", depending on the type of boat.

The lyrics printed here are taken not from the old riverboat song, but from its reincarnation as a capstan shanty out at sea. But some features remain that distinguish it from the usual shanty structure, and that capture the essence of the original slave song. The shanty's particular vibrancy and energy is partly thanks to the quickfire call-and-response pattern within the first line of each chorus ("Rollin'! *Rollin'!* Rollin'! *Rollin'!*"). This alternation between soloist and chorus creates a real sense of unity and dynamism on board – giving the singers a much-needed morale boost, given the unimaginably dreadful conditions that slaves endured.

GOODBYE, FARE YE WELL

Hey boys! Oh, don't you hear the old man say?
Goodbye, fare ye well! Goodbye, fare ye well!
Oh, don't you hear the old man say?
Hurrah, me boys! We're homeward bound!

We're homeward bound to Liverpool town
Goodbye, fare ye well! Goodbye, fare ye well!
Where all them Judies, they will come down
Hurrah, me boys! We're homeward bound!

And when we gits to the Wallasey Gates
Goodbye, fare ye well! Goodbye, fare ye well!
Sally and Polly for their flash
    men do wait
*Hurrah, me boys! We're homeward
    bound!*

And one to the other ye'll hear
    them say
*Goodbye, fare ye well! Goodbye,
    fare ye well!*
"Here comes Johnny with his
    fourteen months' pay!"
*Hurrah, me boys! We're homeward
    bound!*

We meet these fly gals and well ring the old bell
Goodbye, fare ye well! Goodbye, fare ye well!
With them Judies, we'll raise merry hell
Hurrah, me boys! We're homeward bound!

We're homeward bound to the gals o' the tom
Goodbye, fare ye well! Goodbye, fare ye well!
And stamp up me bullies and heave it around
Hurrah, me boys! We're homeward bound!

And when we get home, boys, oh, won't we fly
   round
Goodbye, fare ye well! Goodbye, fare ye well!
We'll heave up the anchor to this bully sound
Hurrah, me boys! We're homeward bound!

We're all homeward bound for the old backyard
Goodbye, fare ye well! Goodbye, fare ye well!
Then heave, me bullies, we're all homeward
   bound
Hurrah, me boys! We're homeward bound!

Heave with a will boys, oh, heave long and
   strong
Goodbye, fare ye well! Goodbye, fare ye well!
Sing a good chorus, for 'tis a good song
Hurrah, me boys! We're homeward bound!

We're homeward bound, we'll have yous to
   know
Goodbye, fare ye well! Goodbye, fare ye well!
And over the water to England must go!
Hurrah, me boys! We're homeward bound!

With its buoyant, dance-like feel, this shanty will get
stuck in your head for hours at a time. Composed in
three-time, its lilting rhythm conveys real excitement
at the prospect of leaving the ship behind and
stepping ashore. Returning home after a long journey

brought with it the chance to go out and have a good time, with a whole trip's wages in your pocket.

The "old man" saying goodbye to the sailors is the ship's captain, whose strict rules and harsh discipline the sailors can't wait to leave behind. As they approach Wallasey – at the mouth of the River Mersey, on the homeward approach to Liverpool – they look forward to the sight of the women coming to welcome their boyfriends ("flash men") home.

When they meet them on land, they will "ring the old bell": that is, they'll go to the pub, and stay till last orders, when the barman would ring the bell, like they

still do today. The bell also served another purpose back then, though: when someone wanted to buy a round of drinks, they would ring the bell to signal their intention – and loud cheers would follow. Sailors with sudden freedom and money to spend would presumably be as ready as anyone to ring the bell, to show off and spoil their loved ones on their return home. This shanty captures that spirit of spontaneity and generosity better than any other.

AND NOW FOR MY SONGS...

RING DING (A SCOTSMAN'S STORY)

Written by: Nathan Evans, Mike Cross & Amy Wadge

I met a girl one Friday night in a bar in Glasgow
   town
she poured me up a whiskey and she told me to
   sit down
we talked all through the night until the sun
   began to rise
and I knew my heart was hers when I looked
   into her eyes

Ring-ding-did-a-little-la-di-oh, ring-di-diddly-
   eye-oh
well I knew my heart was hers when I looked
   into her eyes

She had some airs and graces from a high class
   part of town
and talked about the places that she'd want to
   travel round
And I was scared ask if she would come along
   with me
cos I know that I'd be punching she's a 9 and
   I'm a 3

Ring-ding-did-a-little-la-di-oh, ring-di-diddly-
eye-oh
But I know that I'd be punching she's a 9 and
I'm a 3

I borrowed all the money that my Dad was
saving by
she told me that she wants to see the deserts in
Dubai
Then we went to Barcelona, Paris, Venice, Rome
I was happy with my true love a million miles
away from home

Ring-ding-did-a-little-la-di-oh, ring-di-diddly-
eye-oh
I was happy with my true love a million miles
from home

The savings dwindled quickly but I didn't tell
her so
1,000 other places where my girl wanted to go
so I just played along till, all my cashflow it was
gone
She said "I've got some money, you go home I'll
carry on"

Ring-ding-did-a-little-la-di-oh, ring-di-diddly-
  eye-oh
She said "I've got some money you go home I'll
  carry on"

So now I'm back in Glasgow thinking of what
  could have been
keep checking on her pictures, see the places I
  should have seen
so I think if there's a lesson that you need to
  learn from me
don't act bigger than you are, take a girl from a
  random bar, around the world, stray just to
  far, without a credit card

Ring-ding-did-a-little-la-di-oh, ring-di-diddly-
  eye-oh
well don't act bigger than you are without a
  credit card

TOLD YOU SO

Written by: Nathan Evans, Alan Jukes,
Ross Hamilton & Stephen Jukes

I said, "One day, this world will take you down
And, oh, it can swallow you whole"
I said, "One day, oh boy, you're gonna drown"
I don't wanna say, "I told you so"
Hate to say, "I told you so"

I've been trying to tell you
Tryna warn you, but you won't let go
Sometimes, it's better that you move on
But you just ain't willing to go

I've been thinking
Your ship is sinking and it's far, too far to swim
    to shore
Take my hand, and I'll lead you back to land
'Cause I don't wanna leave you here alone

Oh, I said, "One day, this world will take you down
And, oh, it can swallow you whole"
I said, "One day, oh boy, you're gonna drown"
I don't wanna say, "I told you so"
Hate to say, "I told you so"
Oh hate to say, "I told you so"

I've been trying to tell you
Tryna show you the road back home
But you just don't wanna listen
Now you're spinning out of control

I've been thinking
Your ship is sinking and it's far, too far to swim
    to shore
Take my hand, and I'll lead you back to land
'Cause I don't wanna leave you here alone

Oh, I said, "One day, this world will take you
    down
And, oh, it could swallow you whole"
I said, "One day, oh boy, you're gonna drown"
I don't wanna say, "I told you so"
Hate to say, "I told you so"
Oh hate to say, "I told you so"
Oh-oh-oh-oh-oh

I've been thinking
Your ship is sinking and it's far, too far to swim
    to shore
Take my hand, and I'll lead you back to land
'Cause I don't wanna leave you here alone

Oh, I said, "One day, this world will take you
    down
And, oh, it can swallow you whole" (it can
    swallow you whole)
I said, "One day, oh boy, you're gonna drown"
I don't wanna say, "I told you so"
Hate to say, "I told you so"
Oh hate to say, "I told you so"
Oh-oh-oh-oh-oh

Hate to say, "I told you so"

BIBLIOGRAPHY

The following books, websites and musical groups were an immense help in the research for this book. They provide invaluable insights into the history, purpose and meaning of the shanties. Particular thanks also to the shanty collectors Stan Hugill, Cecil Sharp and Neil Colquhoun, who put so many of these songs to paper before they disappeared.

Hugill, Stan. *Shanties from the Seven Seas: Shipboard Work-Songs and Songs Used as Work-Songs from the Great Days of Sail.* Connecticut: Mystic Seaport, 1994.

Hugill, Stan. *Shanties and Sailors' Songs.* London: Herbert Jenkins, 1969.

Sharp, Cecil. *English Folk-Chanteys.* London, Simpkin, Marshall, Hamilton, Kent & Co., 1914.

Smyth, Gerry. *Sailor Song: The Shanties and Ballads of the High Seas.* London: The British Library, 2021.

Terry, Richard Runciman. *The Shanty Book: Sailor Shanties.* London: J. Curwen & Sons, 1926.

Kimber's Men *www.kimbersmen.com*

London Sea Shanty Collective *www.londonseashantycollective.com*

Storm Weather Shanty Choir *www.shantychoir.com*

The Exmouth Shanty Men *www.exmouthshantymen.com*

The Fisherman's Friends *www.thefishermansfriends.com*

The Jovial Crew *www.thejovialcrew.com*

The Longest Johns *www.thelongestjohns.com*

The Roaring Trowmen *www.roaringtrowmen.co.uk*

The Longest Song Wiki *thelongestsong.fandom.com*

BBC News *www.bbc.co.uk*

BBC Science Focus *www.sciencefocus.com*

Contemplations from the Mariana Trench *www.contemplator.com*

Historic UK *www.historic-uk.com*

Mainly Norfolk: English Folk and Other Good Music *www.mainlynorfolk.info*

New York Times *www.nytimes.com*

New Zealand Folk Song *www.folksong.org.nz*

Sailor Songs *www.sailorsongs.com*

San Francisco Maritime National Park Association *www.maritime.org*

Shanties and Sea Songs *www.shanty.rendance.org*
Sing Shanties Blog *www.singshanties.blogspot.com*
Terre Celtiche (Celtic Lands) Blog *www.terreceltiche.altervista.org*
The Guardian *www.theguardian.com*
The Spectator *www.spectator.co.uk*
Wikipedia *www.wikipedia.org*

ABOUT THE AUTHOR

Nathan Evans first gained fame in 2020, when he posted videos of himself singing sea shanties on social media service Tiktok, triggering a surge of interest in sea shanties. In 2021, he released a cover version of the 19th-century shanty 'Wellerman' which reached number-one in the UK Singles Chart and also charted and went platinum status in several other countries. His growing music career led him to leave his job as a postal worker.

In 2021, he released his own arrangement of the 19th-century shanty of the now multi-platinum 'Wellerman' which went number-one in the nine countries including the UK and has achieved over one and a half billion streams to date.

In January 2021, Evans signed a recording contract with Polydor Records, a music publishing deal with Sony Publishing, and to Professor Jonathan Shalit's InterTalent for Management and UTA as his live booking agent.

This is his first book.

ILLUSTRATIONS BY SALLY TAYLOR

WELBECK

PUBLISHING GROUP

Love books? Join the club.

Sign up and choose your preferred genres to receive tailored news, deals, extracts, author interviews and more about your next favourite read.

From heart-racing thrillers to award-winning historical fiction, through to must-read music tomes, beautiful picture books and delightful gift ideas, Welbeck is proud to publish titles that suit every taste.

bit.ly/welbeckpublishing